BLESSING YOUR CHILDREN

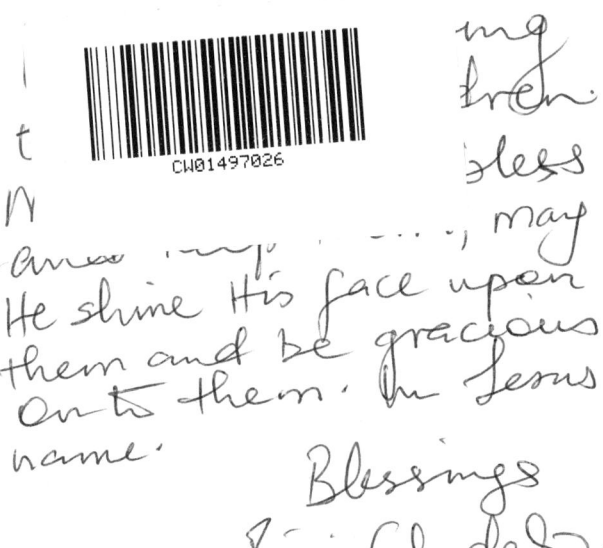

my
bren.
bless
... ..., may
He shine His face upon
them and be gracious
onto them. In Jesus
name.

Blessings
Bisi Abadeso.

BLESSING YOUR CHILDREN

*31 Days of Declaring
God's Word Over
Your Children*

BISI GBADEBO

Blessing Your Children

ISBN: 978-1-9162317-0-2

"The Lord bless you and keep you;
The Lord make His face shine upon you,
and be gracious to you; the Lord lift up His
countenance upon you, and give you peace."

Numbers 6 v 24-26

DEDICATION

This book is dedicated to my Praying
Parents family and all Parents that are
committed to blessing and declaring God's
Word over their children lives.

CONTENTS

FOREWORD

I am so delighted Sis Bisi has turned the **"Blessing Your Children** - 31 days of Declaring God's Word Over Your Children" which we completed in the Praying Parent group into a book.

Her consistency in supporting and encouraging parents to pray and support their children in practical ways, especially for busy families has been invaluable. I am always so encouraged and refreshed every time I go into the Praying Parents Facebook group.

All areas of life are covered through the declarations/blessings and several months after completing the 31 days of declarations I go back to my collated list to declare over my children.

The way she has combined a number of verses together and provides where to say your child(ren)'s names out loud in particular makes them even more powerful.

I would encourage all parents to consider using these declarations/blessings daily; either reading all declarations daily or focusing on specific ones for a period of time.

This book will definitely be a blessing to your family.

~ Diane Oredope PhD

Blessing Your Children - 31 days of Declaring God's Word Over Your Children reminds me of what the bible says about death and life being in the power of the tongue (Proverbs 18:21). In this book, each declaration is an opportunity to partner with God and speak HIS plan and purpose for my children into existence, to align their lives with the vision and plan designed for them by God.

Just like God spoke into existence and created our world, each day that we speak God's word over our children, we are shaping their lives and their world. This is what I experienced with this 31 Day Blessing and Declaration book, and it will be your experience too.

This book is full of proclamations of God's absolute truth concerning our children and His truth makes the power and lies of the enemy ineffective! The declarations in this book are biblical, therefore as you speak them, a demand is placed upon Heaven to attend to your words and bring God's perfect will into your children's lives, because God watches over His words to perform them. Halleluyah!

~ Kemi Oyin-Adeniji

INTRODUCTION

Are you blessing your children?

As parents, one of the best things we can do for our children is to bless and declare the word of God over their lives every day. When we bless our children we are calling out the greatness in them, we are prophesying into their lives, into their future, and into their destiny. The Word of God says death and life are in the power of the tongue.

> *Death and life are in the power of the tongue, and those who love it will eat its fruit. (Proverbs 18 v 21)*

> *Pleasant words are like a honeycomb, sweetness to the soul and health to the bones. (Proverbs 16 v 24)*

Our tongue has incredible power, it has the power to give death or life, therefore, as parents, we should be very careful of what we speak into our children's lives. The words we declare into our children's lives are like seeds that germinate and produce after its kind. They can either affect them positively or negatively. Our speech should be full of grace and seasoned with salt (Colossians 4 v 6), that it may minister grace to the hearer (Ephesians 4 v 29). Our words should build and not tear down.

We should use our tongue to speak life, to bring life, and to give life. When we use it to bless and speak God's promises into our children's lives, we are shaping their destiny and future to be aligned with the will and the purpose of God for their lives. By blessing and declaring the promises of God into and over our children's lives, we are affirming them, we are telling them that we believe in them, that they are created for a purpose, that they are loved, valuable and unique. We are empowering them to prosper and fulfil their destiny. And those words shall not return void, they will accomplish and achieve God's plans and purposes for their lives in Jesus name.

For as the rain comes down, and the snow from heaven, and do not return there,

but water the earth, and make it bring forth and bud, that it may give seed to the sower and bread to the eater, so shall My word be that goes forth from My mouth; it shall not return to Me void, but it shall accomplish what I please, and it shall prosper in the thing for which I sent it. (Isaiah 55 v 10-11)

The same way the rain and snow waters the earth and help the seed to grow and produce fruit, so will the word of God that we declare into our children's lives, the word will not return empty, but will bring life, growth and produce fruits in their lives. Fruits of greatness, success, health, righteousness, salvation, promotion, advancement, peace, joy and love.

This book **Blessing Your Children** is a 31 days of declaring God's word over your children and grandchildren's lives. One for each day of the month, each blessing is based on the promises of God in the Bible, with scripture references at the end of each blessing. The blessings are not only meant to be declared for 31 days, continue to speak them over your children regularly or on a daily basis.

At the end of this book, I have also included a blessing specifically for your sons and daughters. You can add to the blessing when pronouncing it over your child as led by the Holy Spirit. Personalise it, declaring into specific areas of their lives, depending on their age, gifts/talents, character, academic and career pathway, profession, personality, and relationships. In Genesis 49 v 28 Jacob blessed his twelve sons, blessing each one with "the blessing appropriate to him."

You can also declare any of these blessings on special occasions or important milestones in your child's life.

THE POWER OF
SPOKEN WORD

In the book of Genesis 1 v 1-3

*In the beginning God created the heavens
and the earth. The earth was without form,
and void; and darkness was on the face of
the deep. And the Spirit of God was hover-
ing over the face of the waters. Then God
said, "Let there be light" and there was light.*

God said "Let there be light and there was
light" —that is the power of the spoken word
in demonstration right there. He spoke to
that darkness and there was light!. If God
had not spoken those words, the earth would
have remained the same – formless and
empty; with the deep ocean still engulfed in
darkness.

The word of God has the power to trans-
form darkness to light, it can turn situations
around. Things shift in the atmosphere when
we declare God's word. We should, therefore, declare His Word into every dark

situation in our lives and family's with bold-ness and confidence; believing that whatsoever we say shall come to pass. As we begin to declare God's word over our children, we will see changes, transformation, healing, de-liverance, restoration, and reconciliation. The word of God has the power to set free, to deliver, make whole and shape destinies.

> In Mark 11 v 12: *Now the next day, when they had come out from Bethany, He was hungry. And seeing from afar a fig tree having leaves, He went to see if perhaps He would find something on it. When He came to it, He found nothing but leaves, for it was not the season for figs. In response Je-sus said to it, "Let no one eat fruit from you ever again." And His disciples heard it.*

Jesus cursed the fig tree and the following day as they went passed the tree…

Mark 11 v 20-23.

> *Now in the morning, as they passed by, they saw the fig tree dried up from the*

roots. And Peter, remembering, said to Him, "Rabbi, look! The fig tree which You cursed has withered away."

So Jesus answered and said to them, "Have faith in God. For assuredly, I say to you, whoever says to this mountain, 'Be removed and be cast into the sea,' and does not doubt in his heart, but believes that those things he says will be done, he will have whatever he says.

The power of the spoken word, Jesus is telling us here that when we speak to any situation and do not doubt but believe, we will have whatever we say. So also, when we bless our children by declaring God's word over their lives and do not doubt but believe, those words will come to pass in their lives. Let us, therefore, be careful not to speak negative words over our children especially when angry. Don't underestimate the power of your words and in the promises of God that you declare over your children. Your words have a great impact on the lives of your children.

In the book of Judges Chapter 6 v 11-12,

> *Now the Angel of the Lord came and sat under the terebinth tree which was in Ophrah, which belonged to Joash the Abi-ezrite, while his son Gideon threshed wheat in the winepress, in order to hide it from the Midianites. And the Angel of the Lord appeared to him, and said to him, "The Lord is with you, you mighty man of valour.*

The angel of the Lord appeared unto Gideon and called him a mighty man of valour. Gideon did not believe in himself, he did not see himself has a mighty man of valour, he was afraid of the Midianites, he saw himself as weak and the least in his father's house. He said to the angel...

> *So he said to Him, "O my Lord, how can I save Israel? Indeed my clan is the weakest in Manasseh, and I am the least in my father's house."*

The angel spoke God's word over Gideon, he called him a mighty man of valour, he spoke into his future, which activated what was inside Gideon. He already had the potential but needed someone to declare, affirm and call it forth. The words he heard strengthen his faith, he went out and fulfilled God's calling and purpose for his life.

Your children need to hear you bless, affirm and declare God promises into their lives. They need to hear who God created them to be, what they can accomplish through Him, and His plans and purposes for their lives. Your words of declaration and blessings will dispel their fears and insecurities. Your words will help clear their pathway and shape their future. Your words will build up their confidence and their faith in God. It will empower them to see themselves as God sees them – As a chosen generation, a royal priesthood, a holy nation, God's special people. (1 Peter 2 v 9)

BLESSING

Blessing your children is pronouncing or imparting God's words in the form of prayer into their lives. It means to speak favourably about them and to affirm, commend and validate them. It helps them understand their worth and your love for them. By blessing your children, you are empowering them to prosper and fulfil God's purpose for their lives.

God established the tradition of blessing His people.

In Genesis 1 v 28, God blessed Adam and Eve.

> *Then God blessed them, and God said to them, "Be fruitful and multiply; fill the earth and subdue it; have dominion over the fish of the sea, over the birds of the air, and over every living thing that moves on the earth."*

The first thing that God did after creating Adam and Eve was to bless them to be fruitful, multiply, fill the earth, subdue and have dominion. And this blessing came to pass in their lives. They were fruitful, multiplied and replenish the earth.

He blessed Abraham saying…

> *I will make you a great nation; I will bless you and make your name great; and you shall be a blessing. I will bless those who bless you, and I will curse him who curses you; and in you all the families of the earth shall be blessed." Genesis 12 v 2-3*

> *I will make you exceedingly fruitful; and I will make nations of you, and kings shall come from you. And I will establish My covenant between Me and you and your descendants after you in their generations, for an everlasting covenant, to be God to you and your descendants after you. Also I give to you and your descendants after you the land in which you are a stranger, all the land of Canaan, as an everlasting possession; and I will be their God." Genesis 17 v 6-8*

He also blessed Noah and his sons after the flood in Genesis 9 v 1. *So God blessed Noah and his sons, and said to them: "Be fruitful and multiply, and fill the earth.*

In Genesis 27 v 28-29, Isaac blessed Jacob and those declarations came to pass in Jacob's life. Jacob blessed his twelve sons and prophesied into their future (Genesis 49). We can read evidence of the fulfillment of some of these prophecies in the Bible.

God spoke to Moses to tell Aaron and his sons to bless the children of Israel saying…

> *"The Lord bless you and keep you; the Lord make His face shine upon you, and be gracious to you; the LORD lift up His countenance upon you, and give you peace."*

> *So they shall put My name on the children of Israel, and I will bless them." Numbers 6 v 24-27*

God wants His children to live a blessed life, and He has given you the responsibility as the spiritual authority over your children to bless them regularly and when you declare His promises over your children, God will surely bless them as He promised in His word.

Jesus also blessed the children in Mark 10 v 13-16.

I encourage you to be intentional about speaking blessings and God's promises over your children regularly. May those words accomplish what you desire and bear much fruit in their lives in Jesus name. We have been given the responsibility as parents to speak life over our children and what the word of God says about them.

HOW TO BLESS YOUR CHILDREN

• Declare It Out Loud

Blessing and declaring God's word aloud over your children is life-transforming and powerful. You are activating the word of God to begin to work on your children's behalf. Your words release God's supernatural power upon them. In the Bible, as written above, God blessed Adam and Eve, Abraham, and Noah by verbalising the blessings. Jacobs also blessed his sons and grandchildren by declaring the blessings out. I encourage you to speak these blessings out loud enough for your child to hear you as you declare it over his/her life.

And God will do exceedingly and abundantly above all that you ask or think according to His mighty power at work within you. Ephesians 3 v 20.

• Laying Of Hands

You can bless your children by laying your hands on them as you speak out these blessings. You may lay your hands on their head or shoulder, hold their hands or give them a hug and declare the blessing. Genesis 48 v 14 – Here we read Jacob laid his hands on Joseph's sons to bless them.

Jesus in the book of Mark 10 v 13–16 laid hands on the children and blessed them.

> *Then they brought little children to Him, that He might touch them; but the disciples rebuked those who brought them. But when Jesus saw it, He was greatly displeased and said to them, "Let the little children come to me, and do not forbid them; for of such is the kingdom of God. Assuredly, I say to you, whoever does not receive the kingdom of God as a little child will by no means enter it." And He took them up in His arms, laid His hands on them, and blessed them.*

- **Voice/Video Recording/ Social Media or Telephone**

Send the blessing to your children and grand-children as a voice message or through video recording. You can also call and declare the blessing over the phone, or connect with them and bless them through different social media medium such as skype, facetime, or any other social media means of communication. Let them hear your voice as you declare these blessings.

- **Declare It By Faith:**

Declare the blessings by faith, believing that the words you declare shall come to pass in your child's life. Mark 11 v 23. And he/she shall surely be blessed. Genesis 27 v 33.

- **Declare It With Authority**

And I will give you the keys of the kingdom of heaven, and whatever you bind on earth will be bound in heaven, and whatever you loose on earth will be loosed in heaven. Matthew 16 v 19

God has given you the authority to bind and loose, use the authority you have in Christ Jesus to declare these blessings into your child's life.

• **Write It Out**

You can also bless your child by writing out the blessing, especially if your child is grown and no longer lives with you. Write out the blessing and send it by text or email to them.

• **Attach High Value to Your Words**

Attach great importance to your words as you declare blessing over your child. As we read earlier, the Angel of the Lord prophesied into Gideon's future by calling him a "mighty man of valour", when Gideon saw himself as weak. The Angel prophesied into Gideon's future by calling him a man of courage, tenacity, fearless and bold. Those words inspired and empowered Gideon, he believed the words and started to also see himself as courageous, fearless, tenacious and bold.

See the potential – the talents, gifts, in your child and declare it. Let them know how valuable they are. How highly you think of them and their future. Help them see and know their worth through the words that you speak over them. Let them know they are of great worth.

• Invest In their Future

As a parent, it's your responsibility to discover, nurture and develop your child's gifts and talents. Identify what your child's strength and abilities are, and support him/her in developing those gifts and talents.

Invest in their lives by :

Speaking words of encouragement and blessing over them.

Calling out those gifts through words of affirmation and blessing.

Show interest in what they love doing or good at and support their development in that area.

Provide learning opportunities for them to develop their gifts and talents.

Support them by providing the necessary tools and equipment needed.

Be there to take them for necessary trainings and competitions.

Be there to cheer them on.

Understand and listen to them.

Guide and correct them.

Praying for them.

As you declare these blessings over your children, my prayer is that God will honour His words and bless your children. These blessings and declarations will accomplish what you have sent it forth to do in the lives of your children and grandchildren. May it encourage, affirm, commend, restore and build up their faith in the Lord. May these blessings and declarations inspire and empower them to fulfill their purpose and become who God has called them to be in Jesus name.

Day One

LOVE GOD/SALVATION

*Jesus answered him, "The first of all the
commandments is: 'Hear, O Israel, the Lord
our God, the Lord is one. And you shall love
the Lord your God with all your heart, with
all your soul, with all your mind, and with all
your strength.' (Mark 12 v 29-30)*

Blessing and Declaration

I declare that you [insert your child's name] will know God, love Him and serve Him with all your heart, with all your soul, with all your mind, and with all your strength. Above all else, seek God's kingdom and righteousness and all other things He will provide for you. May you believe in Jesus and declare Him as your Lord and Saviour. May you serve and worship Him in spirit and in truth.

May you be strong in the Lord and in the power of His might. May you,[insert your child's name] daily experience the constant and lasting love, joy, peace and the freedom that comes only through knowing and having a personal relationship with Jesus Christ. I pray and declare that nothing shall be able to separate you from the love of God which is in Christ Jesus our Lord in Jesus name, Amen.

Matthew 6 v 33; Mark 12 v 29-30; Romans 8 v 39; 10 v 9; Galatians 5 v 1; Ephesian 6 v 10.

Day Two

REDEEMED

Christ has redeemed us from the curse of the law, having become a curse for us (for it is written, "Cursed is everyone who hangs on a tree"), that the blessing of Abraham might come upon the Gentiles in Christ Jesus, that we might receive the promise of the Spirit through faith. (Galatians 3 v 13-14)

Blessing and Declaration

Christ has redeemed you [insert your child's name] from the curse of the law. You have been redeemed from sin, poverty, sickness, and diseases. You are the redeemed of the Lord. You have been set free from the works and plans of the enemy by the blood of Jesus. The mark of the blood of Jesus is upon you. I cover you with the blood of Jesus. The law of the spirit that brings life in Christ Jesus has set you free from the law of sin and death.

I declare that you are blessed; God will enlarge your coast and make your name great just as He did for Abraham. You will prosper in every way and be in good health physically, spiritually and emotionally. Abundant life is yours through Christ Jesus. In Jesus name I declare, Amen.

Genesis 12 v 2; John 8 v 32 & 36;10 v 10; Ephesians 1 v 7; James 1 v 25; 3 John 1 v 2.

Day Three

WORD OF GOD

Your word is a lamp to my feet and a light to my path. (Psalm 119 v 105)

Blessing and Declaration

I declare upon your life today [insert your child's name] that the word of God will be a lamp to your feet and a light that will continually guide your pathway. God's light will lead and direct you in the way of truth. His light will flood your heart and mind, so that you may come into a deeper understanding of His word.

May you not depart from that way of truth, but may you desire and delight in God's word, and treasure it more than silver or gold. May the truth of God's word be firmly established in your heart. May you meditate on His word day and night, may it will bring you light, good health, joy and happiness. Your ways shall be prosperous and you shall succeed in all you do in Jesus name, Amen.

Joshua 1 v 8; Psalm 119 v 9- 11 & 105; Proverbs 4 v 22.

Day Four

PLANS AND PURPOSE

For I know the thoughts that I think toward you, says the Lord, thoughts of peace and not of evil, to give you a future and a hope.
(Jeremiah 29 v 11)

Blessing and Declaration

I declare upon your life today [insert your child's name] that God's plans and purpose for your life shall be fulfilled. You have been equipped and qualified to accomplish all that God has called you to do. You will achieve all the great things He planned for your life. They will not be delayed or aborted in Jesus name.

May you have a healthy sense of purpose, and clarity of what God has called you to do. May you walk in God's perfect will for your life and always be in the centre of God's will all the days of your life. His counsel shall stand concerning you in Jesus name. May you live a life of significance and of purpose in Jesus mighty name, Amen.

Proverbs 19 v 21; Jeremiah 29 v 11.

Day Five

HEAR GOD VOICE

Your ears shall hear a word behind you, saying, "This is the way, walk in it,"

Whenever you turn to the right hand or whenever you turn to the left. (Isaiah 30 v 21)

Blessing and Declaration

You, my child {insert your child's name] will hear and recognise the voice of the Good Shepherd and follow Him, the voice of a stranger you will not hear or follow. You will not be distracted, but sensitive and attentive to the voice of the Holy Spirit.

May the Lord anoint your ears to hear Him as He speaks to you and your heart to receive His word. You will hear the voice of the Holy Spirit clearly above all others, saying "This is the way, walk in it". The Holy Spirit will instruct, teach and lead you in the way you should go. You will not miss your way or your purpose in life in Jesus name, Amen.

Psalm 32 v 8; Proverbs 4 v 20; 19 v 20; Isaiah 30 v 21; John 10 v 2-5 & 27.

Day Six

WISDOM

*The Spirit of the Lord shall rest upon Him,
the Spirit of wisdom and understanding,*

*The Spirit of counsel and might, the Spirit of
knowledge and of the fear of the Lord.*

(Isaiah 11 v 2)

Blessing and Declaration

I declare that the Spirit of the Lord is upon you [insert your child's name] the Spirit of wisdom and understanding, the Spirit of counsel and might, the Spirit of knowledge and the fear of the Lord. I pray the Holy Spirit will make you wise in the knowledge of God and His word; and in all that you set out to do in life. May He teach and guide you into all truth and show you things to come.

May you be blessed with the wisdom of God that is pure, peaceable, considerate, that is willing to put others first, full of mercy, good fruit, impartial and sincere. May you embrace wisdom and understanding, may it preserve and keep you. May wisdom promote and bring you honour, and may it set a crown glory upon your head.

My child, do not be wise in your own eyes, put your trust in the Lord always. I bless you with wisdom to make wise choices in life, to live, walk, and speak wisely. May you be wise beyond your years and walk in the fear of the

Lord. May you know exactly what He has called you to do and discover the glorious blessings He has in store for you. May it be said of you that the Spirit of God is in you and that you have insight, understanding and excellent wisdom in Jesus name.

Daniel 5 v 14; Psalm 119 v 99-100; Proverbs 4 v 9; 9 v 10-12; Isaiah 11 v 2; Ephesians 1 v 17-18; James 3 v 17.

Day Seven

COURAGE

*Be strong and of good courage, do not fear
nor be afraid of them; for the Lord your God,
He is the One who goes with you. He will not
leave you nor forsake you."
(Deuteronomy 31 v 6)*

Blessing and Declaration

My child (insert your child's name) I bless and declare upon your life today, may you be strong and be of good courage, because God is with you. He will never leave nor forsake you. He will always be with you because He lives in you. May you have the courage to stand for what is right, be confident and un-ashamed to speak the truth and declare God's word.

I pray that you will always trust in the Lord with all your heart and not depend on your own knowledge or way of doing things. May you always listen for God's voice in every-thing you do and everywhere you go, may He guide you on the right path and give you great success in all your endeavours in Jesus name, Amen.

Deuteronomy 31 v 6; Joshua 1 v 6-7; 1 Chronicles 28 v 20; Proverbs 3 v 5-6; 2 Timothy 1 v 7-8.

Day Eight

FEARFULLY AND WONDERFULLY MADE

I will praise You, for I am fearfully and wonderfully made; marvellous are Your works,

and that my soul knows very well.
(Psalm 139 v 14)

Blessing and Declaration

You [insert your child's name] are God's special child, you are unique, beautiful, and fearfully and wonderfully made in God's image. You are precious in God's sight and are the apple of His eyes, You are God's masterpiece created in Christ Jesus to do great things. You are a chosen generation, a royal priesthood, a holy nation, God's special possession.

May you be like a beautiful crown in the hand of the Lord and a royal diadem in the hand of your God. May you find and know your true worth and identity in Christ. I declare, may your life constantly radiate God's light, love, and glory in Jesus name, Amen.

Psalm 139 v 14; Isaiah 62 v 3; Ephesians 2 v 10; 1 Peter 2 v 9.

Day Nine

GODLY CHARACTER

He shall be like a tree planted by the rivers of water, that brings forth its fruit in its season, whose leaf also shall not wither; and whatever he does shall prosper. (Psalm 1 v 3)

Declaration and Blessing

I declare that you [insert your child's name] are like a tree planted by the rivers of water, that bears fruit at the right time. Fruit of love, joy, peace, patience, kindness, goodness, faithfulness, gentleness and self-control. May these godly character qualities be evident in your life and to all around you. May you always be kind and compassionate to others, forgiving them just as God through Christ forgave you.

May your root go deep into the River of Life (the Lord Jesus) always drawing from the living water daily. Your leaves will not wither - but will be ever green, you will be nourished, refreshed and renewed daily. You will not cease from bearing fruits and may you prosper in all you do - spirit, soul and body in Jesus name, Amen.

Psalm 1 v 3; Jeremiah 17 v 7-8; Galatians 5 v 22-23; Ephesians 4 v 32.

Day Ten

FAVOUR

*For You, O Lord, will bless the righteous;
with favour You will surround him as with
a shield. (Psalm 5 v 12)*

Declaration and Blessing

I declare that you [insert your child's name] are blessed and highly favoured. The favour of God envelopes and surround you as a shield. You will find favour in the sight of God and man. The favour of God will over-flow in your life, may it will bring you before people that will propel you towards your God-given assignment, those that will help you fulfil destiny.

Just like Joseph and Daniel, the favour of God will bring you before Kings and Queens, it will make a way for you where there seems to be no way. The favour of God upon your life will cause doors of op-portunity to open for you, it will speak on your behalf in the mighty name of Jesus name, Amen.

Genesis 39 v 3-4; 41 v 1-57; Psalm 5 v 12; Isaiah 43 v 19; Daniel 1 v 1-21; Luke 1 v 28.

Day Eleven

GRACE

*And God is able to make all grace abound
toward you, that you, always having all
sufficiency in all things, may have an
abundance for every good work.
(2 Corinthians 9 v 8)*

Blessing and Declaration

Insert your child's name] May the grace of God abound toward you so that you will always have more than enough to share with others. May you continue to grow in grace and in the knowledge of our Lord and Saviour Jesus Christ. May God's grace make a way for you, may it open doors of opportunities for you, and may it speak on your behalf.

May God's grace attract the right people into your life, may it cause people to help and favour you. May His grace cause you to stand out above your peers. May you be full of grace and truth just like Jesus. May you be strong and empowered in the grace that is in Christ Jesus. I declare His grace is sufficient for you always in Jesus name, Amen.

John 1 v 14; 2 Corinthians 12 v 9; 2 Timothy 2 v 1; 2 Peter 3 v 18.

Day Twelve

PEACE

*And let the peace of God rule in your hearts,
to which also you were called in one body;
and be thankful. (Colossians 3 v 15)*

Blessing and Declaration

[insert your child's name] May the peace of God which is far beyond human understanding guard your heart and mind in Christ Jesus. The Lord will extend peace to you like a river, and the glory of the nations like an overflowing stream. Your home will be peaceful, safe and secure.

I declare that the peace of God reign and rule in your heart, mind and life. Great shall be your peace for you are taught of the Lord. You will be safe from oppression, it shall be far from you and terror shall not come near you, your home and family. Nothing will make you afraid. You will always be at peace because the Greater one abides with you and lives in you in Jesus name, Amen.

Isaiah 32 v 18; 54 v 13-14; 66 v 12; Philippians 4 v 7; Colossians 3 v 16.

Day Thirteen

PROVISION

The Lord is my shepherd, I shall not want.
(Psalm 23 v 1)

Blessing and Declaration

I bless you [insert your child's name] today
my child and declare; The Lord is your shepherd [insert your child's name] you have
everything you need, you will lack nothing,
you will have more than enough to share
with those in need. For God blesses and
prospers a generous person.

May the Lord give you rest in green pastures.
May He lead you to calm restful waters. You
will always be at peace because you have the
Most High on your side.

May He renew your strength, and lead you
on paths that are right for His namesake.
Even if you walk through a very dark valley,
you will not be afraid because the Lord is
with you. You do not need to worry or be
anxious because the Shepherd of your soul
will continually be your guide.

His rod and shepherd's staff will protect and
comfort you. May He prepare a banquet for
you in front of your enemies. May He anoint

your head with oil, and your cup will over-
flow with blessings. Surely His goodness and
mercy will be with you all the days of your
life and you will live in the house of the Lord
forever and ever in Jesus name I declare, Amen.

Psalm 23 v 1-6; Proverbs 11 v 25; 22 v 9.

Day Fourteen

ORDERED STEPS

*The steps of a good man are ordered by the
LORD, and He delights in his way.
(Psalm 37 v 23)*

Blessing and Declaration

[Insert your child's name] I declare that your steps are being ordered and directed by the Lord because He delights in every detail of your life. May He continually guide your step and lead you in the way you should go. May you always commit your ways and plans to the Lord and allow Him to lead and guide you.

My child, happy is the person who does not walk in step with wicked people, may you not associate with such people or follow their advice. May you always be in the right place at the right time. Every day of your life, may you walk in the path that Jesus Christ wants you to walk in. May you walk in God's perfect will for your life,

May you live and walk in a manner worthy of the Lord, fully pleasing Him in all your ways. You will not stumble or fall. You will mount up with wings as an eagle, you will walk and not grow weary, you will run and not faint. You will walk in victory in every area of your life in Jesus name, Amen.

Psalm 16 v 11; 37 v 23; 119 v 133; Proverbs 3 v 6; Isaiah 40 v 3; Colossians 1 v 10.

Day Fifteen

GIFTS AND TALENTS

As each one has received a gift, minister it to one another, as good stewards of the manifold grace of God. (1 Peter 4 v 10)

Blessing and Declaration

I declare you [insert your child's name] are gifted and talented, may you be diligent and committed to developing your gifts and talents, may you use them to be a blessing to others and for God's glory. Your gifts and talent will open doors of opportunities for you. God's purpose for your life shall be fulfilled.

I pray for courage and strength to step out in faith to fulfill your divine assignment. You will not lag behind, you will not hide or bury your gift and talent but use it to further God's kingdom. I declare upon your life today, that your greatness shall be released and destiny fulfilled in Jesus name, Amen.

Matthew 25 v 14-30; Romans 12 v 6-8; 1 Peter 4 v 10; James 1 v 17.

Day Sixteen

ARISE AND SHINE

Arise, shine; for your light has come!

And the glory of the Lord is risen upon you.
(Isaiah 60 v 1)

Blessing and Declaration

[Insert your child's name], Arise and shine for your light has come; for the glory of the LORD is risen upon you. The light of the LORD will shine on you; the brightness of his presence will be with you. Your light will shine for all to see. You will not conform to the ways of the world, but you will be a beckon of light and hope to those around you.

Nations will be drawn to your light, and kings to the brightness of your rising. You shall be a shining example to your generation and generations to come. A light that radiates love, joy, peace, patience, kindness, goodness, gentleness and self-control. Your light will shine in such a way that people will see Jesus Christ in you and be drawn to God. Your light and life will impact others for good in Jesus mighty name, Amen.

Isaiah 60 v 1-3; Matthew 5 v 14-16; Galatians 5 v 22-23.

Day Seventeen

GRACIOUS WORDS

For the Lord gives wisdom; from His mouth
come knowledge and understanding.
(Proverbs 2 v 6)

Blessing and Declaration

I declare that you [Insert your child's name] will speak of excellent things, and from your lips will come what is right; your mouth will speak truth; wickedness is an abomination to your lips. All the words of your mouth are with righteousness, nothing is false or misleading in them. Your words shall give life, hope, and build others up.

May the words that come out of your mouth be kind and helpful words, may your words inspire, encourage and give grace to those who hear them. May your words be always with grace, seasoned with salt, so that you may know how to answer everyone. May you always say the right words at the right time. Your mouth shall always speak words of wisdom, knowledge, and understanding in Jesus name, Amen.

Psalm 49 v 3; Proverbs 2 v 6; 8 v 6-8; 16 v 24; Ephesians 4 v 29; Colossians 4 v 6.

Day Eighteen

LORD YOUR HELPER

My help comes from the Lord, who made heaven and earth (Psalm 121 v 2)

Blessing and Declaration

[Insert your child's name], the Lord is your Helper and Protector, your Refuge and Fortress, your Redeemer and the horn of your salvation. The Maker of the heavens and the earth is your Helper, He will send you help when you need it. You will never lack helpers in life. Your destiny helpers will locate you. I declare upon your life today that you will not stumble because He who watches over you [insert your child's name] does not slumber nor sleep.

The Lord will always be with you, He will never leave nor forsake you. The sun will not harm you during the day, and the moon cannot harm you at night. The Lord will protect you from all danger, He will keep watch over your life; He will continually watch over your going out and coming in both now and forevermore in Jesus name, Amen.

Deuteronomy 31 v 6; Psalm 18 v 1-2; 121 v 1-8.

Day Nineteen

EXCEL AND PROSPER

*And the LORD will make you the head and
not the tail; you shall be above only, and not
be beneath, if you heed the commandments of
the LORD your God, which I command you
today, and are careful to observe them.
(Deuteronomy 28 v 13)*

Blessing and Declaration

[insert your child's name], I declare upon your life today, you are the head and not the tail, above only and not beneath. You will always move upwards and never downwards. The anointing to excel and prosper rest upon you. You will excel in your studies, at your job, in your business, career, ministry and in every area of your life. You will succeed in all you set your hands to do that is God's will for your life.

May the Lord bless you and be with you in all that you do; may He enlarge your territory and sphere of influence and keep you safe from harm. May the blessings of the Lord that enrich without any sorrow be your portion in Jesus name, Amen.

Deuteronomy 28 v 13; 1 Chronicles 4 v 10; Proverbs 10 v 22.

Day Twenty

RENEWED STRENGTH

But those who wait on the LORD shall renew their strength; they shall mount up with wings like eagles, they shall run and not be weary, they shall walk and not faint.
(Isaiah 40 v 31)

Blessing and Declaration

My dear child, {insert your child's name], the Lord Almighty is your refuge and strength. Always trust in the Lord for help and He will renew your strength. His strength is made perfect in your weaknesses. Out of God's glorious riches, may He empower you with inner strength through His Spirit so that Christ will make His home in your heart through faith.

May He give you the spiritual and physical strength you need to live a life of victory. You will soar high on wings like an eagle. You will run and you will not grow weary, you will walk and you will not faint for His grace is sufficient for you.

May He make your feet as sure as those of a deer, which does not stumble and lead you safely on the steep mountains. May He equip and empower you with the ability and skills you need to overcome every obstacle in life. His grace to overcome all challenges in life is sufficient for you. May you be strong in the Lord and in the power of His might in Jesus name, Amen.

Psalm 18 v 29 & 33; 46 v 1; Isaiah 40 v 31; Habakkuk 3 v 19; 2 Corinthians 12 v 9; Ephesians 3 v 16-17; 6 v 10; Philippians 4 v 13.

Day Twenty-One

GOD YOUR DELIVERER

*Call upon Me in the day of trouble, I will
deliver you, and you shall glorify Me.
(Psalm 50 v 1)*

Blessing and Declaration

[insert your child's name] May the Lord answer you when you call, may the name of the God of Jacob protect and keep you safe from harm. May He send you supernatural help from His Holy place. May He defend and sustain you. May He accept all your offerings and be pleased with all your sacrifices. May He give you your heart desires and make all your plans succeed.

May we (your parents) rejoice with you at your victory and raise a victory banner in the name of our God. May the Lord answer all your prayers and provide everything you need according to His riches in glory. He will give you, His anointed, victory in every area of your life. He will answer from His holy heaven and save you with His mighty strong hand. May you boast and trust in the Lord your God all the days of your life. You will arise and stand up strong for your help comes from the Lord the Maker of heaven and earth. May He answer you whenever you call upon Him in Jesus name.

Psalm 20 v 1- 9; 121 v 2; 145 v 19; Philippians 4 v 19.

Day Twenty-Two

VICTORY

*You are of God, little children, and have
overcome them, because He who is in you is
greater than he who is in the world.*
(1 John 4 v 4)

Blessing and Declaration

I declare upon you today [insert your child's name], you are an overcomer, for greater is He that is in you than he that is in the world. You will overcome all obstacle in life, overwhelming victory is yours through Christ Jesus who loved you and gave Himself for you. You shall not be moved for the Lord is your Rock, Fortress and Deliverer.

I declare victory over your life, victory over sin, victory over sickness, victory over unbelief, victory over poverty, victory over death in Jesus name. May you walk and live a victorious life. You overcome by the blood of Jesus and by the words of your testimony in Jesus mighty name, Amen.

1 Corinthians 15 v 57; 2 Corinthians 2 v 14; Romans 8 v 37; 1 John 4 v 4; 5 v 4; Revelation 12 v 11.

Day Twenty-Three

INTEGRITY

*A good name is to be chosen rather than
great riches, loving favour rather than
silver and gold. (Proverbs 22 v 1)*

Blessing and Declaration

May you [insert your child's name] live a life of integrity and honesty. May integrity and uprightness keep you safe and secure. May you walk blamelessly, always doing what is right, even when no one is watching and speak the truth even when it hurts.

May the Lord keep you from dishonest ways and friends. May you only associate with honesty and trustworthy friends. May God give you the strength of character to speak the truth at all times and develop in you the grace and integrity that only comes through Christ Jesus. May He build greatness in you by developing your character. May you walk before the Lord with integrity of heart all the days of your life. And may the words of your mouth and the meditation of your heart be acceptable in God's sight in Jesus name, Amen.

Psalm 19 v 14; 25 v 12; 119 v 29; Proverbs 10 v 9; 22 v 1, Luke 16 v 10.

Day Twenty-Four

HONOUR YOUR FATHER AND MOTHER

Honour your father and your mother, as the Lord your God has commanded you, that your days may be long, and that it may be well with you in the land which the Lord your God is giving you. (Deuteronomy 5 v 16)

Blessing and Declaration

May you [insert your child's name] honour and obey your father and mother so that all may be well with you and that you may live long on the earth; for this is well pleasing to God. May He give you wisdom and show you how to honour, respect, love and bless your parents and those that stand in place of authority over your life. May you honour your parents by obeying their godly instructions and corrections, may you always bring them joy and peace. May the Lord bless you abundantly my child, so that you may provide and care for your parents in their old age.

I declare upon you today [insert name] it shall be well with you my child, the Lord will perfect all that concerns you, you will live long, you will live to a good old age. May you live a long, happy and prosperous life. May you will dwell in peaceable and safe environment in Jesus name, Amen.

Deuteronomy 5 v 16; Exodus 20 v 12; Proverbs 1 v 8; 31 v 28; Ephesians 6 v 2-3; Colossians 3 v 20.

Day Twenty-Five

GOD'S ANOINTED

Saying, "Do not touch My anointed ones, and do My prophets no harm." (Psalm 105 v 15)

Blessing and Declaration

You [insert your child's name] are God's anointed one, you are the apple to His eyes. His Holy Spirit is upon you, He has anointed you to preach the good news about Jesus to the poor, to heal the broken-hearted and comfort those who are sad and announce God's freedom to those that are held captive.

I declare over you today, no weapon formed against you will succeed and every tongue that rises against you in judgment, you shall condemn. All those that gather together against you shall fall for your sake. The Almighty God is on your side, you shall not be moved. He is your Vindicator. He will contend with all those that contend with you. He will fight your battles for you and you shall hold your peace. May He deliver your soul from death, your eyes from tears and your feet from falling. May you walk and see the goodness of the Lord in the land of the living in Jesus name.

Psalm 27 v 13; 35 v 1; 105 v 15; 116 v 8-9; Isaiah 49 v 25; 54 v 15 & 17; 2; 61 v 1-2; Corinthians 1 v 22.

Day Twenty-Six

SOUND MIND

For God has not given us a spirit of fear, but
of power and of love and of a sound mind.
(2 Timothy 1 v 7)

Blessing and Declaration

God has not given you [insert child's name] a spirit of fear, but He has given you the Spirit of power, of love and of a sound mind in Jesus name. You have the mind of Christ. You will not fear or be in dread, for the Almighty God is with you always. I declare over your life that you have the spirit of power, of love and of a calm and well balanced-mind; of discipline and self-control. May your thoughts be fixed on what is true, honourable, right, pure, lovely, and admirable. May you think about things that are excellent and worthy of praise.

May the Holy Spirit fill you with boldness and confidence to speak the word of God and stand for what is right. You are a child of the King, fear has no place or hold over you; you are a strong and courageous child of God. I declare this blessing upon you today in Jesus name.

Joshua 1 v 9; Proverbs 28 v 1; Acts 4 v 29; 1 Corinthians 2 v 16; Philippians 4 v 8; 2 Timothy 1 v 7.

Day Twenty-Seven

LOVE

But above all these things put on love, which is the bond of perfection. Colossians 3 v 14

Blessing and Declaration

[insert your child's name], God loves you so much that He gave His Son Jesus Christ to die for you. And through the Holy Spirit, God's love had been poured out into your heart. May you be rooted and established in God's love, and understand how wide, long, high and deep the love of Christ is. May you know His love that transcends knowledge, so that you may be filled with all the fullness of life and power that comes from God in Jesus name, Amen.

May you abide in His love all the days of your life and may that love radiate and overflow to others. May you love the Lord your God with all of your heart, soul and strength and your neighbour as yourself.

I bless you today and declare that God will bless you with the ability to demonstrate His love to others.

May you be patient, kind and compassionate.

May you show love by not being jealous or envious of others.

May you walk in humility and grace so that God may lift you high.

May you show respect and be considerate of others. Looking out for others interest not just your own.

May you speak words of encouragement and build others up and not tear them down.

May you not hold on to grudges or keep a record of people's wrong but be willing to forgive as Christ forgave you.

May you delight and rejoice in justice and truth.

May you never lose faith or give up, may you be hopeful and continue strong in Jesus name.

May these qualities of love be evident in your life in Jesus name.

Luke 10 v 27; John 3 v 16; Romans 5 v 5; 1 Corinthians 13 v 1-7; Ephesian 3 v 18-19.

Day Twenty-Eight

FRIENDSHIP/ RELATIONSHIPS

He who walks with wise men will be wise,
but the companion of fools will be destroyed.
Proverbs 13 v 20

Blessing and Declaration

My dear child {insert your child's name], may the Lord bless your relationships. May the Lord give you the wisdom to choose your friends wisely. May the Holy Spirit lead and guide you to the right friends and relationships.

May you associate with wise friends so that you may be wiser, friends that will lift you up and not pull you down, friends that sharpen each other as iron sharpens iron. Friends that will influence you for good and you will also influence positively. Wise, loyal, honest, caring and God- fearing friends. May the Lord bring destiny helpers your way, may your destiny helpers locate you and you locate them in Jesus name, Amen.

Genesis 2 v 23-24; Proverbs 1 v 10-19; 13 v 20.

Day Twenty-Nine

PROTECTION

The name of the LORD is a strong tower;
the righteous run to it and are safe.
Proverbs 18 v 10.

Blessing and Declaration

You [insert your child's name] dwell in the secret place of the Most High and abide under the shadow of the Almighty. The Lord God is your refuge, your fortress, and deliverer. His everlasting arms are under you to support you, He will protect and deliver you from danger and from all deadly diseases. He will drive out the enemy before you. He will cover you with his wings; you will be safe in his care; His faithfulness will protect and defend you.

No evil shall befall you, neither shall any disaster come near you or your home. God will give His angels charge over you, to keep watch, defend and protect you wherever you go. The Lord will answer whenever you call on Him, He will always be with you. He will deliver and honour you. He will satisfy you with long life and show you His salvation in Jesus name, Amen.

Deuteronomy 33 v 27; Psalm 18 v 1-3; 34 v 7; 91 v 1-16.

Day Thirty

PROSPERITY AND ABUNDANCE

And all these blessings shall come upon you and overtake you, because you obey the voice of the LORD your God. Deuteronomy 28 v 2.

Blessing and Declaration

You [insert your child's name] are blessed.

I declare you are blessed in the city, blessed in the country, blessed everywhere you go. Your children both born and unborn are blessed. The Lord will bless your land. The country that you live in is blessed with abundant crops, calves, and lambs. Your food is blessed - your kitchen and storehouses are blessed. You are blessed when you go out and when you come in. The Lord will crush and defeat all your enemies who rise up against you. They shall flee from you, never to rise again in Jesus name.

May the Lord bless you with the dew of heaven and the richness of the earth, may He open the windows of heaven and blessed your land with rain in its season. The Lord will bless the work of your hands, your studies, your job, your career, your business, and your bank account are blessed. You will excel in all you set your hands to do.

The Lord will establish you and cause you to prosper in the land that you live in. May He lavish you with goods things. You will lend to nations and you will not need to borrow. The Lord will make you the head in all you do and not the tail, you will always be on top and never at the bottom. Every step you take and every move you make shall lead to out-standing success in Jesus mighty name, Amen.

Genesis 27 v 28; Deuteronomy 28 v 1-14.

Day Thirty-One

BLESSING

Blessed is the man who trusts in the Lord, and whose hope is the Lord. Jeremiah 17 v 7

Blessing and Declaration

[Insert your child's name] May the Lord bless you and keep you, may He shine His face upon you and be gracious on to you. May He lift up His countenance upon you and favour you. May He watch over you and give you peace.

May the grace of our Lord Jesus Christ, the love of God, and the fellowship of the Holy Spirit be with you always. I declare God's goodness and mercy shall follow you all the days of your life and you shall dwell in the house of the Lord forever and ever in Jesus name.

Go forth and fulfill God's purpose for your life. Go forth and be a success. Go forth and maximise your potential. Go forth and maximise the glory and greatness of God upon your life. Go forth and be a blessing to this generation and generations to come. Go forth and fulfill destiny. Go forth my child and shine! In Jesus name, Amen.

Numbers 6 v 24-26; Psalm 23 v 6; 2 Corinthians 13 v 14.

BLESSING FOR YOUR SON

My precious son [insert name] I bless you and declare over you today. You are blessed and highly favoured. You are a child of the Most High God. You are handsome, unique and intelligent. You are perfectly created in God's own image. You are a mighty man of valour, a man after God's own heart. You are my beloved son, in whom I am well pleased.

May you walk before God with integrity of heart. May you continue to increase in wisdom and stature, and find favour with God and all people. You will grow up to love and serve God in spirit and in truth. May you be passionate for about things of God and be an example to others in your words, behaviour, faith, love, and purity.

You will succeed in life and fulfill your God-given destiny. You will succeed in your academics, in your career, profession, in your workplace, in your business, in your marriage and in every area of your life. May the Lord bless the work of your hands. Among the out-standing, you will stand out, for the anointing of excellence is upon you. You will flourish, you will prosper. You will know the right steps to take and the right choices to make in life because the Spirit of God is in you and He will direct and lead you in the way to go.

I pray the Spirit of wisdom, knowledge and understanding rest upon you. May you trust in the Lord always and not in your own un-derstanding. You will not listen to or follow the advice of the wicked. I bless your spirit, soul, and body. The Lord will satisfy you with long life and show you His salvation.

I bless your future wife. May the Lord bless you with a God-fearing spouse You will marry your own wife – a virtuous woman of noble character, the bone of your bone and flesh of your flesh. You will not marry your enemy, you will marry your friend – God chosen one for you. May you love her as Christ loved the church and gave himself up for her. May she be like a fruitful vine flour-ishing within your house. Both of you will live together in peace and harmony. Your home shall be a haven of peace. May it be filled with love, joy, peace, laughter and abundant of God's blessings. You will know how to care for yourself and be the head of your household. I bless your marriage and home.

I bless your children, may they be like olive plants around your table. The Lord will give you the wisdom and the grace to train your children in the way they should go. You will not mourn over your children. You will be present on your children's day of joy, no one will take your place.

I bless your children's children to many generations to come, may you live to see your children's children. I plead the blood of Jesus over your life, I soak you into the blood of the lamb. May the hand of the Lord rest upon you, and may you live in good health all the days of your life. I bless your spirit, soul, and body today my child. I love you son and I declare that it shall be well with you all the days of your life in Jesus name.

BLESSING FOR YOUR DAUGHTER

My dear precious daughter [insert name] I bless you and declare over you today. You are blessed and highly favoured. You are a child of the Most High God. You are unique, beautiful, intelligent and talented. You are a wise woman of great and noble character. Your worth is far more than rubies.

You will be fruitful and you will multiply and eat the good of the land you live in. Lines will fall in pleasant places for you. You will succeed in life, you will prosper and fulfill destiny. May the Lord bless the work of your hands. May you be passionate about the things of God. I pray the Spirit of wisdom, knowledge and understanding rest upon you. May you trust in the Lord with all your heart and not on your own understanding. I bless your spirit, soul, and body. The Lord will satisfy you with long life and show you His salvation.

I bless your future husband. You will marry your own husband, you will not marry your enemy, you will marry your friend – God chosen one for you. A God-fearing man, a man of integrity. May he love you as Christ loves the church and gave himself up for her. Both of you will live together in peace and harmony.

I bless your marriage and home. Your home shall be a haven of peace. May it be filled with love, joy, and laughter. You will know how to care for yourself and your household like the proverbs 31 woman and the bread of idleness you will not eat. The heart of your husband will confidently trust in you, and he will not lack any good thing.

May you be clothed with strength and dignity, and look forward with joy without fear of the future. May you extend your hand to the poor and provide for the needy.

May the Lord give you increase on every side, you and your household. May you be blessed by the Lord, who made heaven and earth.

I bless your children - The Lord will give you the wisdom and the grace to train your children in the way they should go. You will not mourn over your children. You will be present on your children's day of joy, no one will take your place. Your children will honour you, they will rise and call you blessed and your husband will also praise you.

I bless your children's children to many generations to come, may you live to see your children's children. I plead the blood of Jesus over your life, I soak you into the blood of the lamb. May the hand of the Lord rest upon you, and may you live in good health all the days of your life.

I bless your spirit, soul, and body today my child. I love you and declare that it is well with you my daughter [your daughter's name], in Jesus name. Many daughters have done virtuously and excellently well, but you excel them all.

How to contact the author:

blessurchild@gmail.com

Bisi Gbadebo

Lightning Source UK Ltd.
Milton Keynes UK
UKHW020555041119
352859UK00003B/56/P